Alexander Gresbek

Alexander Gresbek

© 2023

Alexander Gresbek

Discovering Spain And The Costa Blanca

*by
Alexander Gresbek*

Discovering Spain And The Costa Blanca

Alexander Gresbek

Welcome to "Discovering Spain and the Costa Blanca," a photobook that takes you on a visual journey through Spain's main cities and its beautiful coastal regions.

Emphasizing the Costa Blanca, located on the southeast coast of Spain, this stunning stretch of coastline boasts crystal-clear waters, pristine beaches, charming villages and vibrant cities. This photobook captures the essence of this region through stunning photographs that showcase its natural beauty, rich history, and unique culture.

Join us on this journey and discover the hidden gems of Spain and the Costa Blanca through the lens of our talented photographer, Alexander Gresbek.

Alexander Gresbek

Discovering Spain and the Costa Blanca | 7

Alexander Gresbek

Alexander Gresbek

Alicante

Alicante, located in the southeastern region of Spain, is a stunning coastal city that offers a perfect blend of history, culture, and modern amenities. The city boasts a warm Mediterranean climate, making it an ideal destination for tourists all year round.

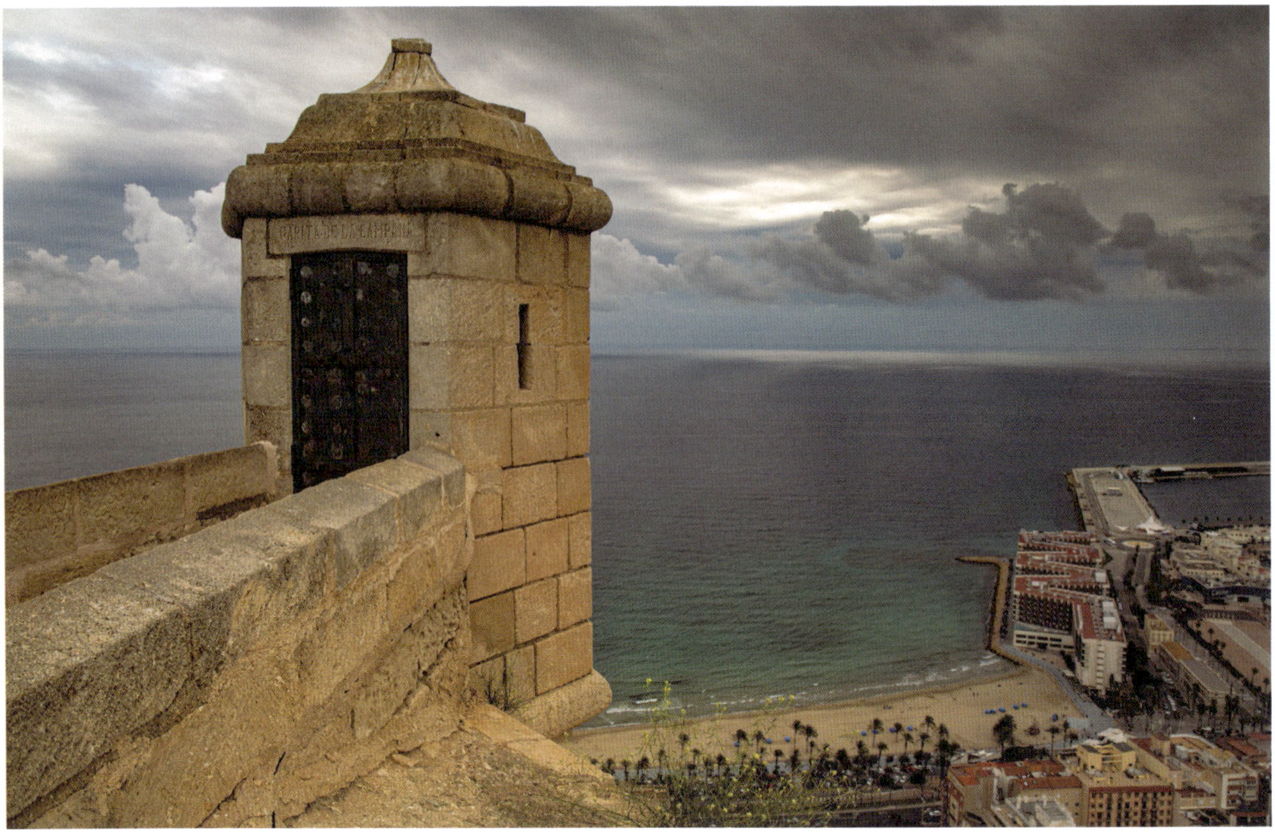

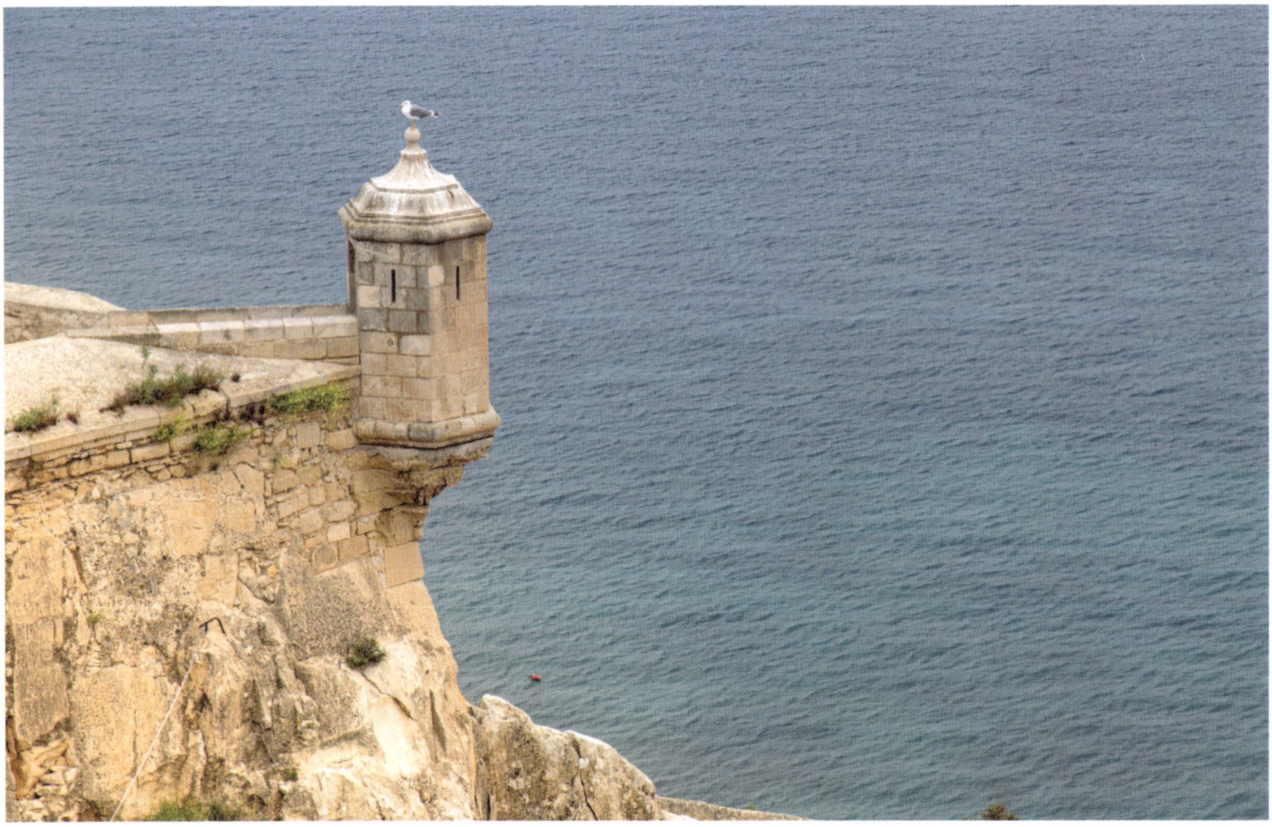

Alexander Gresbek

Santa Barbara Castle, Alicante

The Santa Barbara Castle is a historic fortress located on Mount Benacantil, overlooking the city of Alicante in southeastern Spain. The castle dates back to the 9th century and has served various purposes throughout history, including as a defensive fortress, a prison, and a military base. Today, the castle is a popular tourist attraction and offers stunning panoramic views of the city, the Mediterranean Sea, and the surrounding landscape. Visitors can explore the castle's grounds, including its towers, walls, and courtyards, and learn about its fascinating history through exhibits and guided tours. The castle also hosts various cultural events and exhibitions throughout the year.

Almeria

Almería is a city located in the southeastern part of Spain, on the Mediterranean coast. It is the capital of the province of Almería, which is situated in the autonomous community of Andalusia. Almería has a population of approximately 200,000 people, making it the 16th most populous city in Spain.

The city of Almería is known for its beautiful beaches, historic sites, and unique architecture. It has a rich history, having been inhabited by the Phoenicians, Romans, Moors, and Christians over the centuries. Some of the most popular attractions in Almería include the Alcazaba, a Moorish fortress that dates back to the 10th century, the Cathedral of Almería, which was built in the 16th century, and the Museum of Almería, which showcases the region's history and culture.

Alcazaba of Almería

The Alcazaba of Almería is a Moorish fortress that was built in the 10th century during the Muslim rule of the Iberian Peninsula. It is located on a hill overlooking the city of Almería and the Mediterranean Sea, and it was originally built as a defensive structure to protect the city from attacks by Christian forces.

The Alcazaba is considered one of the best-preserved examples of Moorish military architecture in Spain. It is a large complex of fortified walls, towers, and buildings, with a central courtyard and several gardens. The fortress was constructed using local stone and features intricate details and decorations, such as arches, domes, and decorative tilework.

Over the centuries, the Alcazaba has been modified and expanded by various rulers, including the Catholic Monarchs, who added new structures and defensive features after they conquered the city in 1489. Today, the Alcazaba is open to visitors and is one of the most popular tourist attractions in Almería. Visitors can explore the fortress and its gardens, and enjoy views of the city and the sea from the top of the walls and towers.

Altea

Altea is a picturesque coastal town located on the Costa Blanca, in the province of Alicante, Spain. It is known for its historic old town, which is perched on a hill overlooking the sea. The town has a relaxed atmosphere and is a popular destination for visitors seeking a more authentic and peaceful holiday experience.

The old town of Altea is a maze of narrow cobbled streets, whitewashed houses, and traditional Spanish buildings. It is home to several art galleries, artisan shops, and restaurants, serving local cuisine.

Promenade

In addition to its beaches and historic old town, Altea has a range of other attractions, including a weekly market, a marina, and a promenade lined with palm trees and cafes.

Our Lady of Consolation

The Church of Our Lady of Consolation, also known as the Church of Altea, is a beautiful landmark located in the historic old town of Altea. The church was built in the 19th century and is considered a prime example of Baroque-style architecture in the Valencia region.

The church's striking blue and white tiled dome is a prominent feature of Altea's skyline and can be seen from miles away. The interior of the church is equally impressive, with its ornate altarpiece, intricate wooden carvings, and beautiful stained-glass windows.

The church is dedicated to Our Lady of Consolation, the patron saint of Altea, and is an important religious center in the town. It is a popular destination for visitors who come to admire its architecture and take in the views of the surrounding area from the church's terrace.

Alexander Gresbek

Discovering Spain and the Costa Blanca | **17**

Alexander Gresbek

18 | Discovering Spain and the Costa Blanca

Alexander Gresbek

Alexander Gresbek

Alexander Gresbek

Discovering Spain and the Costa Blanca | **21**

Barcelona

Barcelona is a vibrant city located on the north-eastern coast of Spain. It is renowned for its unique architecture, world-class museums, and rich cultural heritage. The city is also a hub for art, fashion, and cuisine, and offers a range of activities for visitors of all ages and interests.

Alexander Gresbek

Alexander Gresbek

Park Güell

Park Güell is known for its stunning architectural elements, such as the serpentine bench that winds around the edge of the main terrace, the mosaic-covered salamander, and the gingerbread-like houses at the entrance. The park also features lush gardens and panoramic views of the city.

Alexander Gresbek

The Magic Fountain of Montjuïc

This is a large fountain complex located on Montjuïc hill that features a spectacular water, light, and music show. The fountain was built in 1929 for the Universal Exhibition and was later restored in 1992 for the Olympic Games in Barcelona.

Arc de Triomf

The Arc de Triomf in Barcelona is located at the northern end of Passeig de Sant Joan in the Eixample district. It was built as the main access gate for the 1888 Barcelona World Fair and is one of the city's most popular landmarks. The Arc de Triomf was designed by Catalan architect Josep Vilaseca i Casanovas and is made of red brick and stone.

Alexander Gresbek

Sagrada Familia

The Sagrada Familia is a magnificent basilica located in the Eixample district of Barcelona, designed by the famous architect Antoni Gaudi. Construction began in 1882 and is still ongoing, with an expected completion date of 2026. The basilica is renowned for its unique and awe-inspiring design, featuring intricate facades, towering spires, and colorful stained-glass windows that create a breathtaking interplay of light and color. The Sagrada Familia is one of Barcelona's most popular tourist attractions and a must-visit destination for anyone interested in architecture and design.

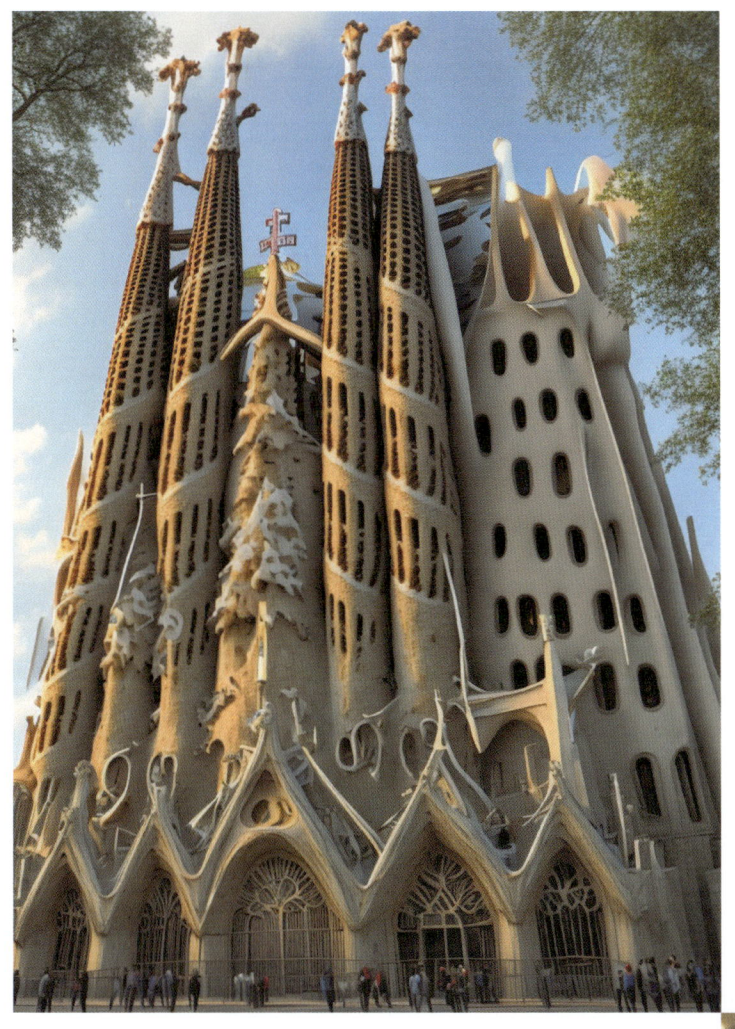

Alexander Gresbek

Antoni Gaudi

Antoni Gaudi i Cornet is a renowned Spanish architect known for his unique and highly individualistic style that is often characterized by the use of curves, vivid colors, and intricate details. Gaudi was born in 1852 in Reus, Catalonia, and is best known for his work on the Sagrada Familia.. He was a key figure in the Catalan Modernisme movement, which emerged in the late 19th century and was characterized by a desire to promote Catalan culture and identity through art and architecture.

Inside the Sagrada Familia

Visitors can explore the interior of the basilica, which is filled with natural light and features a forest of columns that resemble trees. The Sagrada Familia is one of the most popular tourist attractions in Barcelona, and it is highly recommended to book tickets in advance to avoid long queues.

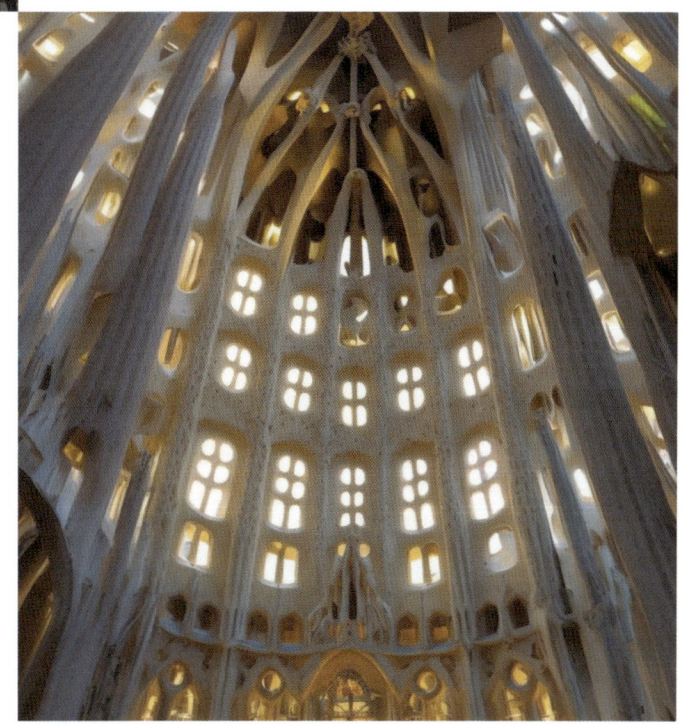

Discovering Spain and the Costa Blanca | 27

Beaches

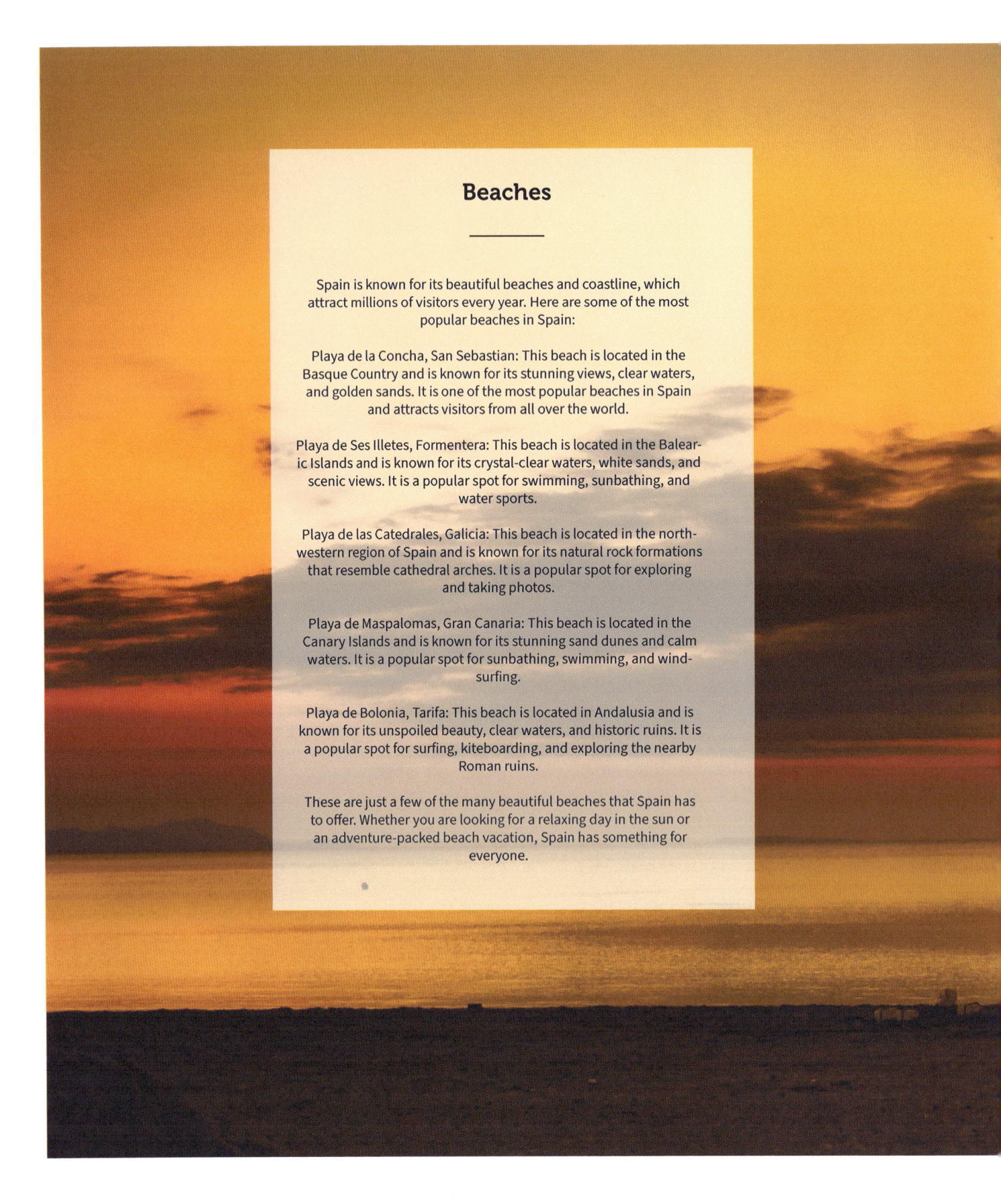

Spain is known for its beautiful beaches and coastline, which attract millions of visitors every year. Here are some of the most popular beaches in Spain:

Playa de la Concha, San Sebastian: This beach is located in the Basque Country and is known for its stunning views, clear waters, and golden sands. It is one of the most popular beaches in Spain and attracts visitors from all over the world.

Playa de Ses Illetes, Formentera: This beach is located in the Balearic Islands and is known for its crystal-clear waters, white sands, and scenic views. It is a popular spot for swimming, sunbathing, and water sports.

Playa de las Catedrales, Galicia: This beach is located in the northwestern region of Spain and is known for its natural rock formations that resemble cathedral arches. It is a popular spot for exploring and taking photos.

Playa de Maspalomas, Gran Canaria: This beach is located in the Canary Islands and is known for its stunning sand dunes and calm waters. It is a popular spot for sunbathing, swimming, and windsurfing.

Playa de Bolonia, Tarifa: This beach is located in Andalusia and is known for its unspoiled beauty, clear waters, and historic ruins. It is a popular spot for surfing, kiteboarding, and exploring the nearby Roman ruins.

These are just a few of the many beautiful beaches that Spain has to offer. Whether you are looking for a relaxing day in the sun or an adventure-packed beach vacation, Spain has something for everyone.

Alexander Gresbek

Coastline

Whether you are looking for a relaxing day on the beach or an adrenaline-filled water sports adventure. The Spanish coastline is one of the longest in Europe, stretching over 8,000 kilometers along the Mediterranean Sea, the Atlantic Ocean, and the Bay of Biscay. The coastline is characterized by its diverse landscapes, including sandy beaches, rugged cliffs, and rocky coves.

Some of the most popular destinations along the Spanish coastline include:

- Costa del Sol: The Costa del Sol is a popular tourist destination in southern Spain, known for its warm weather, sandy beaches, and lively nightlife.

- Costa Brava: The Costa Brava is a rugged coastline in northeastern Spain, famous for its rocky coves, hidden beaches, and clear waters.

- Costa Blanca: The Costa Blanca is located in the eastern part of Spain and is known for its white sandy beaches, crystal-clear waters, and sunny weather.

- Balearic Islands: The Balearic Islands are an archipelago located in the western Mediterranean Sea, known for their beautiful beaches, clear waters, and vibrant nightlife.

- Canary Islands: The Canary Islands are a Spanish archipelago located off the coast of Africa, known for their volcanic landscapes, white sandy beaches, and year-round warm weather.

Overall, the Spanish coastline offers a diverse range of destinations and landscapes for visitors to explore, with something to suit every taste and preference.

Top Beaches Mallorca

Mallorca, also known as Majorca, is the largest island in the Balearic Islands archipelago located in the western Mediterranean Sea. It is a popular destination for beach lovers, with over 200 beaches to choose from. Here are some of the top beaches in Mallorca:

- Cala Agulla: Located in the northeast of the island, Cala Agulla is a long and sandy beach with clear waters and surrounded by pine trees. It is a great spot for swimming, sunbathing, and water sports.

- Playa de Muro: Situated on the north coast of the island, Playa de Muro is a long and wide sandy beach with crystal-clear waters. It is a popular destination for families due to its shallow waters and beachfront amenities.

- Cala Llombards: Located on the southeast coast of the island, Cala Llombards is a small and secluded beach with turquoise waters and a rocky coastline. It is a great spot for snorkeling and diving.

- Es Trenc: Located on the south coast of the island, Es Trenc is a long and sandy beach with turquoise waters and backed by sand dunes. It is a popular destination for sunbathing and swimming.

- Cala Varques: Located on the east coast of the island, Cala Varques is a hidden gem with crystal-clear waters, surrounded by cliffs and pine trees. It is accessible by a short hike and is a great spot for snorkeling.

Overall, Mallorca offers a wide range of beaches, from long and sandy to small and secluded, with crystal-clear waters and stunning scenery. There is something for every type of beachgoer, from families to adventure-seekers.

Benidorm

Benidorm is a popular tourist destination located on the eastern coast of Spain. Known for its high-rise buildings, long sandy beaches, and lively nightlife, it attracts millions of visitors every year.

Alexander Gresbek

Alexander Gresbek

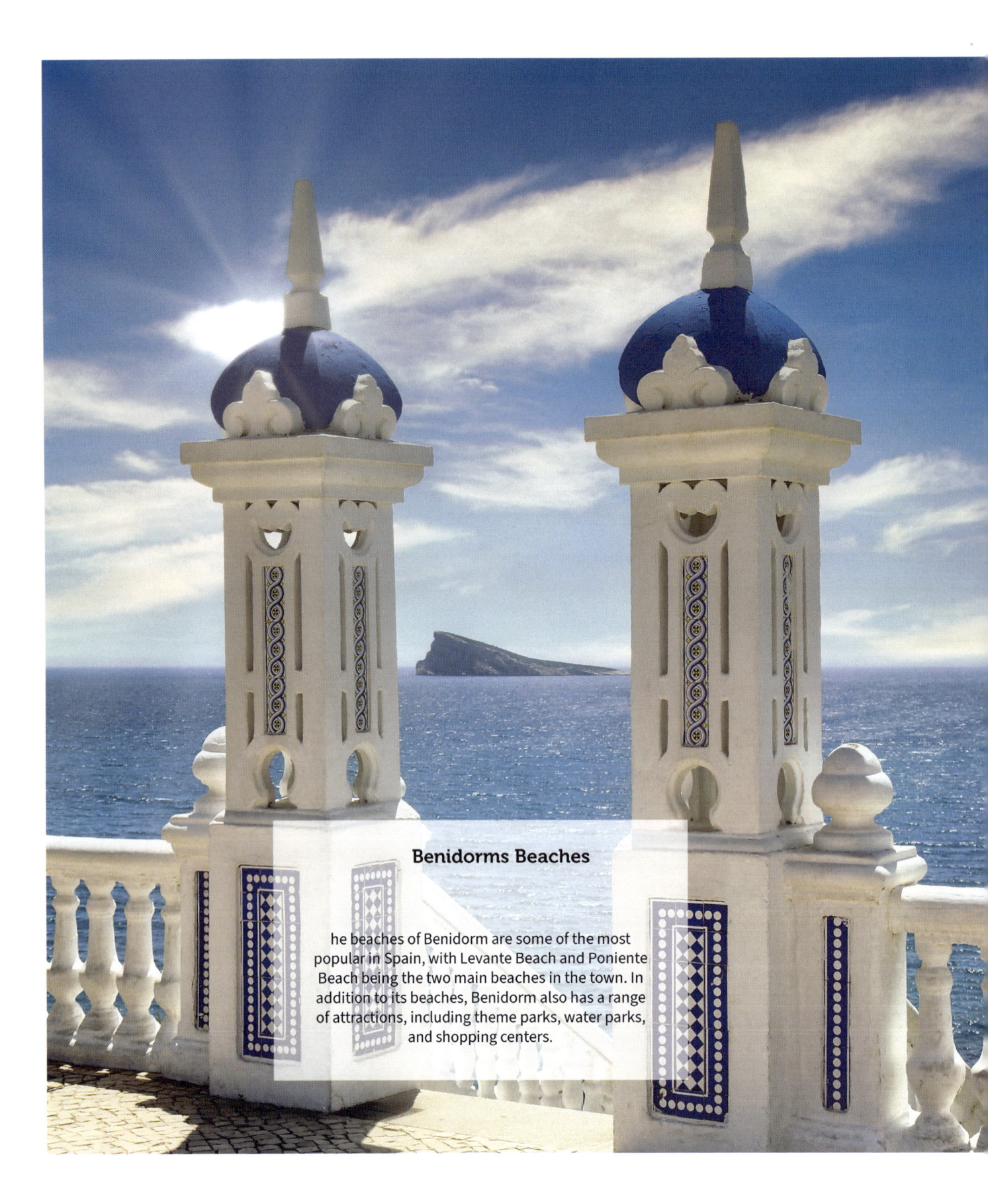

Benidorms Beaches

he beaches of Benidorm are some of the most popular in Spain, with Levante Beach and Poniente Beach being the two main beaches in the town. In addition to its beaches, Benidorm also has a range of attractions, including theme parks, water parks, and shopping centers.

Alexander Gresbek

Old Town

The old town of Benidorm, also known as the historic center, is located on a rocky promontory between the two main beaches, Levante and Poniente. The old town is characterized by narrow streets, traditional houses, and small squares with outdoor cafes and restaurants. It is a charming area to explore, with many historic buildings and landmarks, including the Church of San Jaime and Santa Ana, which dates back to the 18th century.

Nightlife

Benidorm also has a vibrant nightlife, with many bars, clubs, and restaurants offering a range of entertainment and cuisine. The town is known for its British and Irish pubs, as well as its karaoke bars and live music venues.

Discovering Spain and the Costa Blanca | 35

Alexander Gresbek

History

Benidorm has a long history as a fishing village, but it wasn't until the 1960s that it started to become a popular tourist destination. The town's location on the Mediterranean Sea and its warm climate made it an ideal destination for visitors seeking sun, sea, and sand. As the town's popularity grew, more and more hotels and apartments were built, leading to the high-rise skyline that is characteristic of the town today.

Alexander Gresbek

Transformation

In recent years, Benidorm has undergone a transformation, with efforts to improve the town's image and attract a wider range of visitors. This has included improvements to the town's infrastructure, such as a new tram system and improved public spaces, as well as a focus on promoting cultural and ecological tourism.

Alexander Gresbek

Bilbao

Bilbao is a city located in the Basque Country region of northern Spain. It is the largest city in the province of Biscay and the tenth largest in Spain. Bilbao has a population of approximately 350,000 people and is an important cultural, economic, and industrial center in the region.

One of the main attractions in Bilbao is the Guggenheim Museum Bilbao, which is a modern and contemporary art museum designed by architect Frank Gehry. The museum is famous for its unique titanium-clad design and houses a collection of works by artists such as Jeff Koons, Eduardo Chillida, and Richard Serra.

Alexander Gresbek

Frank Gehry

Frank Gehry is a Canadian-American architect who is known for his innovative and groundbreaking designs. Gehry's architecture is characterized by its use of unconventional materials and forms. He is famous for his use of titanium and other metals in his buildings, as well as his incorporation of sweeping, curvilinear shapes that challenge traditional architectural norms.

Calpe

Calpe is a coastal town located on the Costa Blanca in the province of Alicante, Spain. It is known for its beautiful beaches, crystal-clear waters, and stunning natural scenery, including the iconic rock formation known as the Peñón de Ifach.

Alexander Gresbek

Peñón de Ifach

The town has a lively atmosphere and a wide range of attractions, including its beaches, historic old town, and natural parks.

One of the main attractions of Calpe is the Peñón de Ifach, a towering rock formation that rises 332 meters above the sea. The rock is a protected natural park and is home to a diverse range of flora and fauna, including rare bird species. Visitors can hike to the top of the rock, which offers spectacular views of the coastline and surrounding area.

Discovering Spain and the Costa Blanca | 41

Alexander Gresbek

Cartagena

Cartagena is famous for its beautiful architecture, historic landmarks, and cultural attractions. The most notable attraction is the Roman Theater, which was discovered in the 1980s and is now one of the city's most popular tourist sites. Other important landmarks in the city include the impressive Castillo de San Felipe, a fortress built in the 16th century, and the Palacio Consistorial, a stunning baroque-style building that serves as the city hall.

In addition to its historic attractions, Cartagena is also known for its beautiful beaches, crystal-clear waters, and stunning natural scenery. Some of the most popular beaches in the area include La Manga del Mar Menor, Cala Cortina, and Cala Reona. The city also has a vibrant food and drink scene, with many restaurants serving traditional Murcian cuisine, such as paella, seafood, and local wines.

Overall, Cartagena is a beautiful and fascinating city with a rich history and cultural heritage, and it is a must-visit for anyone traveling to the Murcia region of Spain.

Alexander Gresbek

Alexander Gresbek

Alexander Gresbek

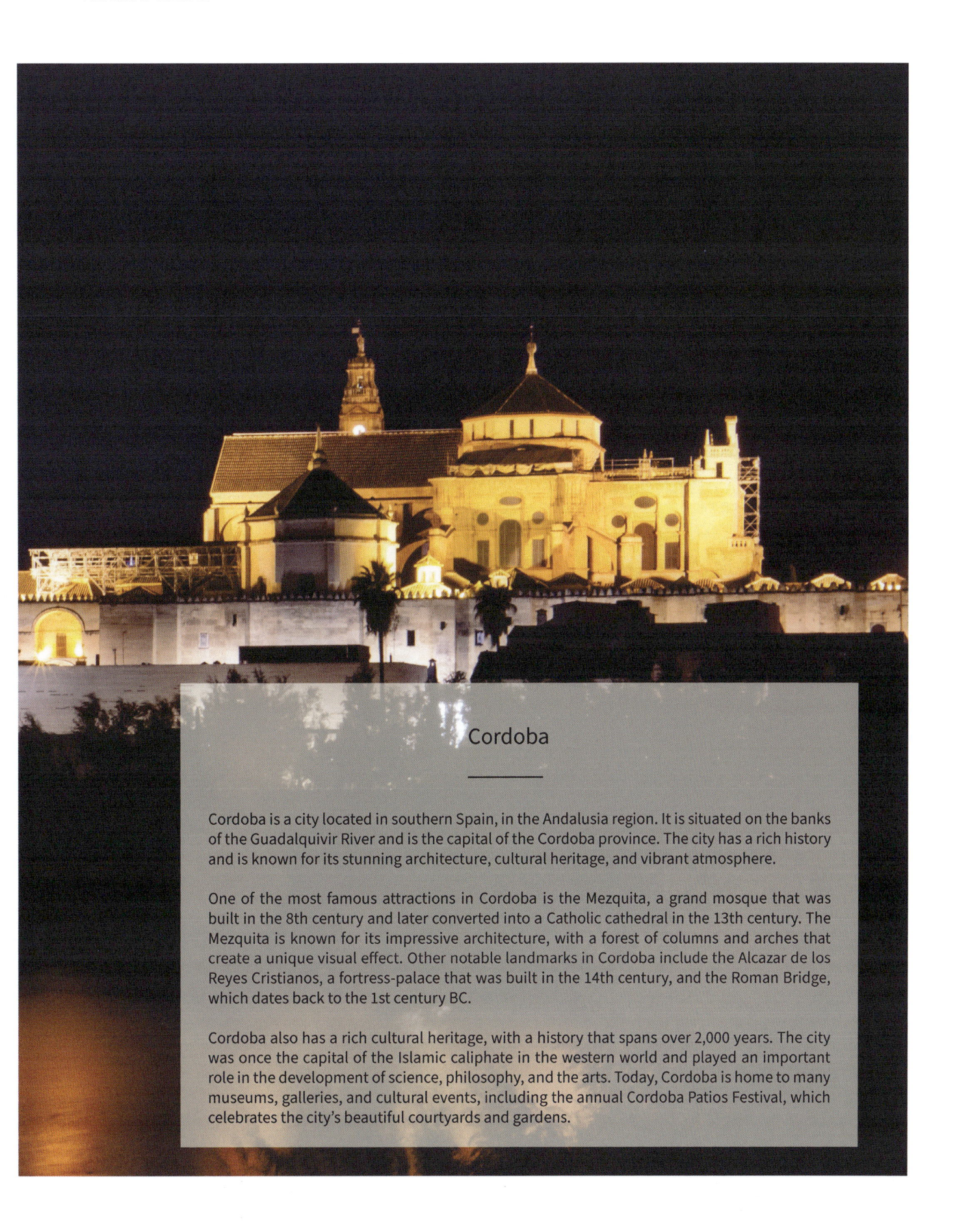

Cordoba

Cordoba is a city located in southern Spain, in the Andalusia region. It is situated on the banks of the Guadalquivir River and is the capital of the Cordoba province. The city has a rich history and is known for its stunning architecture, cultural heritage, and vibrant atmosphere.

One of the most famous attractions in Cordoba is the Mezquita, a grand mosque that was built in the 8th century and later converted into a Catholic cathedral in the 13th century. The Mezquita is known for its impressive architecture, with a forest of columns and arches that create a unique visual effect. Other notable landmarks in Cordoba include the Alcazar de los Reyes Cristianos, a fortress-palace that was built in the 14th century, and the Roman Bridge, which dates back to the 1st century BC.

Cordoba also has a rich cultural heritage, with a history that spans over 2,000 years. The city was once the capital of the Islamic caliphate in the western world and played an important role in the development of science, philosophy, and the arts. Today, Cordoba is home to many museums, galleries, and cultural events, including the annual Cordoba Patios Festival, which celebrates the city's beautiful courtyards and gardens.

Alexander Gresbek

Alexander Gresbek

Costa Blanca

From the French border to the Rock of Gibraltar, the over 1,500 kilometers long coastline is divided into eleven Costas. Generally, the names are more or less successful creations of the respective tourist boards. Even most Spaniards do not know where to assign, for example, the Costa Tropical or the Costa del Garraf. Besides the Costa Brava in the north and the Costa del Sol in the south, the Costa Blanca is one of the coastal sections whose popularity has prevailed. The name Costa Blanca was created by tourism managers in the 1950s. On the one hand, it was supposed to symbolize the traditionally white painted houses, and on the other hand, the lighting conditions that make the sand shine white. Officially, the Costa Blanca begins in Dénia, the northernmost city in the province of Alicante, and ends in Pilar de la Horadada, the southernmost town in the province.

Alexander Gresbek

48 | Discovering Spain and the Costa Blanca

Alexander Gresbek

Discovering Spain and the Costa Blanca | 49

Alexander Gresbek

Alexander Gresbek

Alexander Gresbek

52 | Discovering Spain and the Costa Blanca

Alexander Gresbek

Alexander Gresbek

Alexander Gresbek

Alexander Gresbek

Alexander Gresbek

Denia

Denia has a rich history that dates back to the Roman era, and visitors can still see remnants of its past in the form of the castle that sits atop a hill overlooking the town. The castle was built in the 11th and 12th centuries and served as a fortress to protect against attacks from the sea.

Discovering Spain and the Costa Blanca

Denia´s Castle

The castle dates back to the 11th and 12th centuries, when it was built by the Moors to defend the town against attacks from the sea. After the Reconquista, it was occupied by the Christians and underwent significant renovations to strengthen its defenses.

The castle has a rectangular layout, with a series of towers and walls that enclose an inner courtyard. One of the most notable features of the castle is the Torre del Mig, or Middle Tower, which was added in the 15th century and served as a watchtower and prison.

In addition to its military history, the castle has also been used as a residence for various noble families over the centuries. Today, it is a popular tourist attraction and is open to visitors who can explore the castle's walls, towers, and battlements, and enjoy panoramic views of Denia and the Mediterranean Sea.

Alexander Gresbek

Festivals

Fallas de San José is a festival that is celebrated in Denia and other parts of Spain in March. It is a celebration of spring and involves the creation of large papier-mâché sculptures that are displayed throughout the town. These sculptures, called "fallas," are often satirical or humorous in nature and depict political figures, celebrities, or everyday life.

The sculptures are eventually burned in a spectacular bonfire, which marks the end of the festival. However, one sculpture is typically spared from the flames and is preserved for display in a museum or public space.

Bous a la Mar is another popular festival in Denia that is celebrated in July. It is a bullfighting event that takes place on a special arena that is set up in the town's port. In this event, young men try to grab the bull's horns as it charges towards them. If they are successful, they are lifted out of the water by the crowd, and if not, they fall into the water. This festival has a long history in Denia and is a celebration of the town's maritime traditions.

Coastline

Denia has over 20 kilometers of coastline with a variety of beaches, ranging from quiet coves to bustling sandy stretches. The beaches are perfect for relaxing, sunbathing, and swimming in the Mediterranean Sea.

Alexander Gresbek

Marina

Denia`s Marina is one of the largest marinas in the region.

The marina has a capacity for 546 boats, with berths ranging from 6 to 60 meters in length. It is equipped with modern facilities and services, including water and electricity supply, fuel station, waste collection, and a 24-hour security service.

Denia´s Marina is a popular destination for sailing enthusiasts and offers easy access to nearby beaches and towns.

The marina is surrounded by a lively promenade with a variety of restaurants, cafes, and shops.

Fiestas

Spanish fiestas are an integral part of Spanish culture, celebrated throughout the year in different regions of Spain. These celebrations are typically based on religious, historical, or cultural traditions and involve music, dancing, parades, and fireworks. Examples of Spanish fiestas include La Tomatina, a tomato-throwing festival in Buñol; Semana Santa, a Holy Week celebration held in cities and towns throughout Spain; and San Fermin, a festival in Pamplona famous for the running of the bulls. Other well-known fiestas include Feria de Abril in Seville and La Feria de San Isidro in Madrid. These fiestas are an excellent way to experience the unique and rich culture of Spain and to witness history and traditions come to life through music, dance, and celebration.

Alexander Gresbek

Discovering Spain and the Costa Blanca | **63**

Alexander Gresbek

Guadalest

Guadalest is a picturesque village located in the province of Alicante, Spain. The village is perched on top of a rocky hill and is surrounded by stunning natural scenery, including mountains, forests, and a reservoir. Guadalest is known for its historic buildings, including a castle and several museums, which attract many tourists each year.

Javea

Javea, also known as Xàbia in the local Valencian language, is a charming coastal town located in the northern part of the Costa Blanca region in Spain. It is situated between the towns of Denia and Moraira and is known for its stunning beaches, historic old town, and natural beauty.

Alexander Gresbek

Discovering Spain and the Costa Blanca | 67

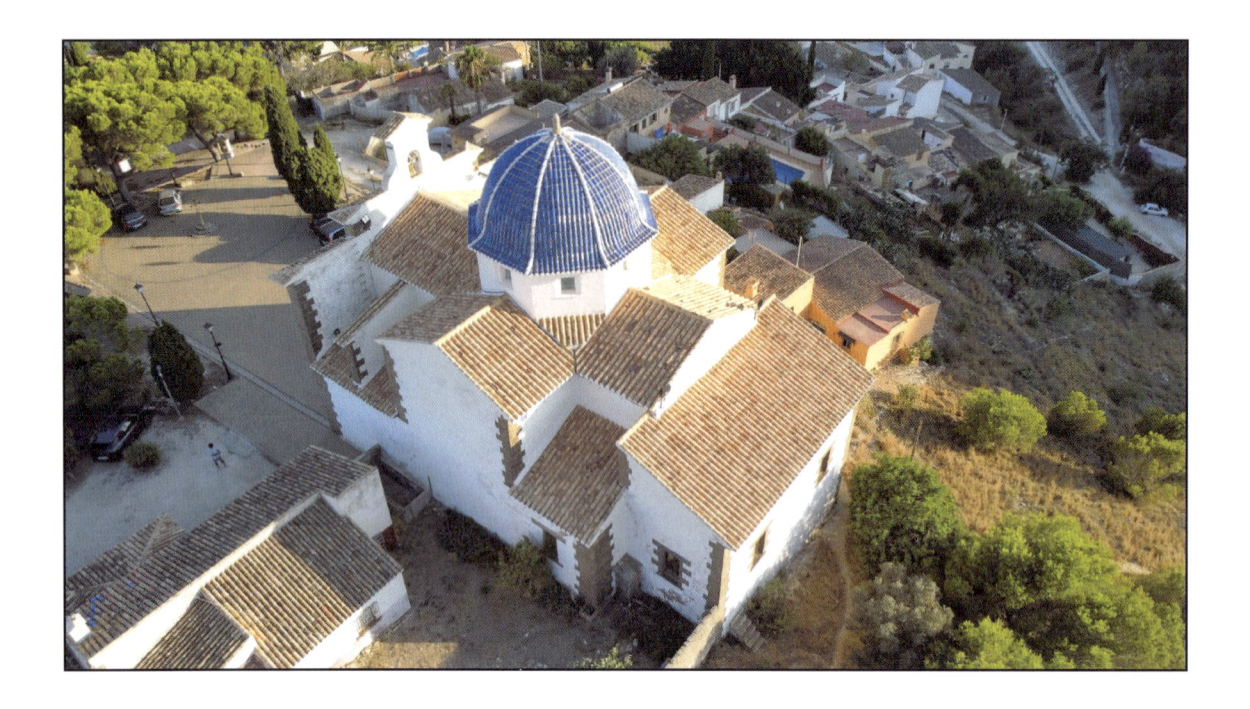

Javea is divided into three main areas: the old town, the port area, and the beach area. The old town is located inland and features historic buildings, narrow streets, and a traditional market square. The port area is located by the sea and is home to a marina, fishing port, and many seafood restaurants. The beach area is located to the south of the town and features sandy beaches, rocky coves, and tourist facilities

Alexander Gresbek

Alexander Gresbek

Alexander Gresbek

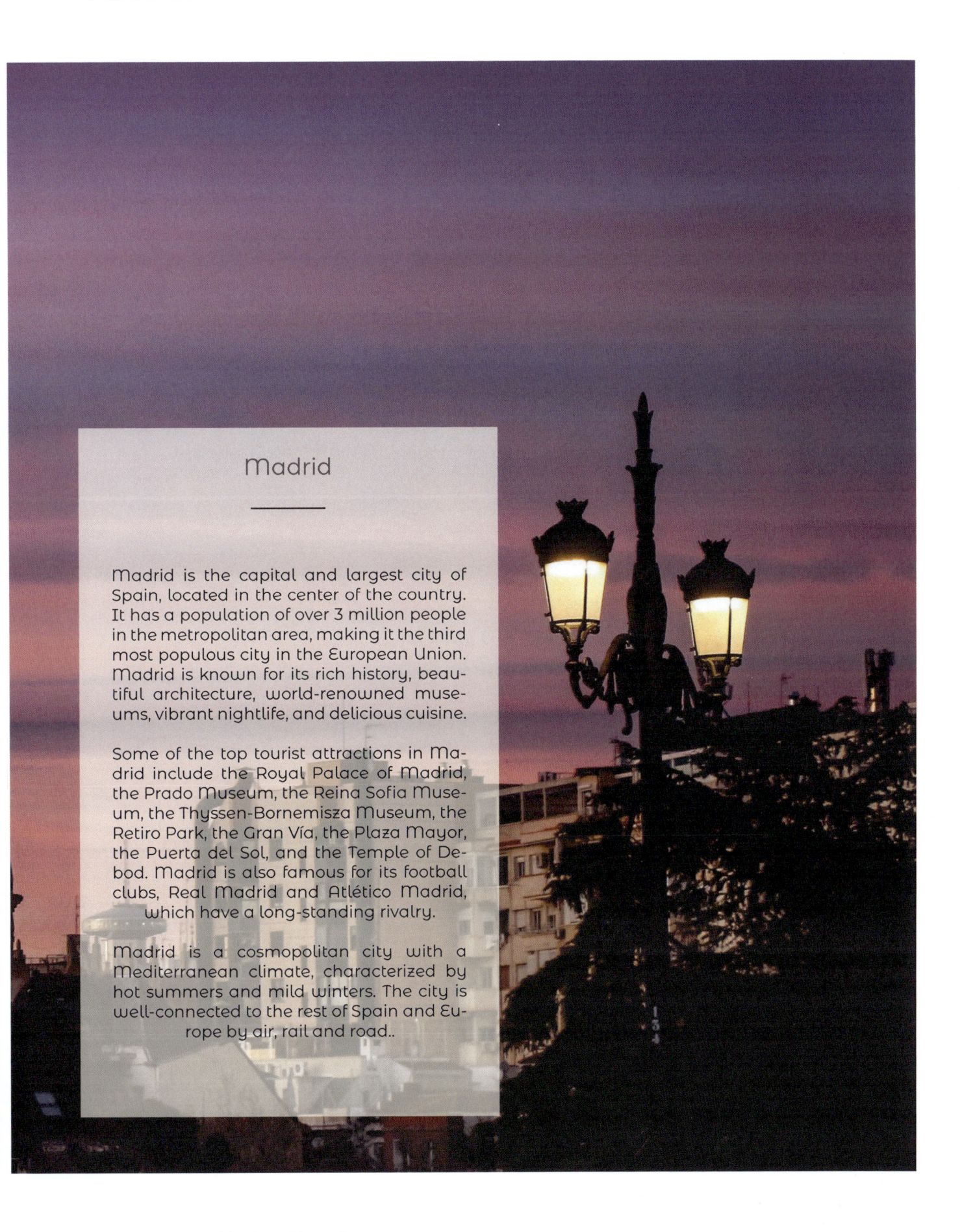

Madrid

Madrid is the capital and largest city of Spain, located in the center of the country. It has a population of over 3 million people in the metropolitan area, making it the third most populous city in the European Union. Madrid is known for its rich history, beautiful architecture, world-renowned museums, vibrant nightlife, and delicious cuisine.

Some of the top tourist attractions in Madrid include the Royal Palace of Madrid, the Prado Museum, the Reina Sofia Museum, the Thyssen-Bornemisza Museum, the Retiro Park, the Gran Vía, the Plaza Mayor, the Puerta del Sol, and the Temple of Debod. Madrid is also famous for its football clubs, Real Madrid and Atlético Madrid, which have a long-standing rivalry.

Madrid is a cosmopolitan city with a Mediterranean climate, characterized by hot summers and mild winters. The city is well-connected to the rest of Spain and Europe by air, rail and road..

Alexander Gresbek

Palace of Madrid

One of the most famous palaces in Madrid is the Royal Palace of Madrid, also known as the Palacio Real de Madrid in Spanish. It is the official residence of the Spanish Royal Family but is only used for state ceremonies and official events. The palace was built in the mid-18th century and is located in the heart of Madrid, near the Plaza de Oriente.

The Royal Palace of Madrid is known for its stunning architecture, grand rooms, and impressive art collections. It has over 3,000 rooms, including state rooms, banquet halls, and private apartments. Visitors can take a tour of the palace and see the grand staircase, Throne Room, Royal Chapel, and other parts of the palace.

Alexander Gresbek

Alexander Gresbek

Alexander Gresbek

Mallorca,

Mallorca, also known as Majorca, is the largest island in the Balearic Islands archipelago, located in the Mediterranean Sea and belonging to Spain. The island has a rich history and culture, with influences from various civilizations, including the Phoenicians, Romans, Moors, and Catalans.

Alexander Gresbek

Alexander Gresbek

Mallorca's Beaches

Mallorca is known for its beautiful beaches. The island's beaches are a mix of long sandy stretches, secluded coves, and rocky cliffs. They are surrounded by crystal-clear waters that are perfect for swimming and snorkeling, and many have soft, white sand that is ideal for sunbathing and relaxing. Mallorca also has many secluded coves that offer a peaceful and tranquil environment away from the crowds. The beaches in Mallorca have facilities such as showers, toilets, sun loungers, and parasols, as well as beach bars and restaurants serving local cuisine.

Moraira

Moraira is a small coastal town located in the province of Alicante, in the Valencian Community region of eastern Spain. It is situated on the Mediterranean Sea and has a population of approximately 9,000 people.

Moraira is known for its beautiful beaches, crystal clear waters, and picturesque scenery. Some of the most popular beaches in Moraira include Playa de l'Ampolla, Playa del Portet, and Platgetes de Moraira. The town is also home to a marina, where visitors can enjoy sailing, fishing, and other water sports.

In addition to its natural beauty, Moraira has a charming old town that features narrow streets, traditional buildings, and a central market square. The town has a rich history, with evidence of human settlement dating back to prehistoric times. Over the centuries, Moraira has been inhabited by Phoenicians, Romans, and Moors, among other cultures, leaving behind a fascinating mix of architectural styles and cultural influences.

Alexander Gresbek

Moraira Castle

The Moraira Castle, from the 18th century, stands in the city center and near the beach. The building, of Bourbon origin, has a floor plan called "ox hoof", that is, semi-circular in shape, and its function, like other buildings of the time, was to protect the inhabitants from the invasions of Berber pirates. These corsairs, coming from Tunisia, Tripoli, Algiers and Morocco, in addition to attacking ships, used to carry out raids or invasions of inland territories in search of Christian slaves.

Alexander Gresbek

Moors and Christians

The Moors and Christians festival is a popular event that takes place in many towns and cities throughout Spain, including Moraira. The festival celebrates the long and complex history of the Iberian Peninsula, which has been shaped by various cultures and civilizations, including the Moors and Christians.

The festival typically involves a series of processions and reenactments that depict key moments in the region's history. Participants dress up in traditional costumes and take on the roles of Moors and Christians, marching through the streets and engaging in mock battles.

In Moraira, the Moors and Christians festival usually takes place in June, and it's one of the town's biggest events of the year.

Mountain Ranges

Spain is home to several mountain ranges, some of which are among the highest peaks in Europe. Here are some of the major mountain ranges in Spain:

- The Pyrenees: This is a range of mountains that runs along the border between Spain and France, stretching for over 430 km. It includes several peaks that are over 3,000 meters, including Aneto, which is the highest peak in the Pyrenees.

- The Sierra Nevada: Located in the southern region of Andalusia, this mountain range is known for its stunning natural beauty, with snow-capped peaks and lush forests. It is home to Mulhacén, the highest peak in mainland Spain, which stands at 3,478 meters.

- The Picos de Europa: These mountains are located in the north of Spain, in the autonomous community of Asturias. They are known for their dramatic cliffs, deep gorges, and stunning vistas. The highest peak in the range is Torre de Cerredo, which stands at 2,650 meters.

- The Sistema Central: This mountain range runs through central Spain and includes several peaks that are over 2,000 meters, including Peñalara, which is the highest peak in the range at 2,428 meters.

- The Cordillera Cantábrica: This range runs along the northern coast of Spain and includes several peaks that are over 2,500 meters. It is known for its rugged terrain, dense forests, and picturesque villages.

These are just a few of the major mountain ranges in Spain, and there are many more that offer stunning scenery and challenging hiking opportunities.

Alexander Gresbek

Alexander Gresbek

Alexander Gresbek

Alexander Gresbek

Alexander Gresbek

Alexander Gresbek

Ronda

Ronda is a city located in the province of Malaga in southern Spain, in the region of Andalusia. It is situated on a plateau overlooking the dramatic El Tajo Gorge and is known for its stunning natural scenery, rich history, and unique architecture.

Alexander Gresbek

Puente Nuevo

One of the most famous attractions in Ronda is the Puente Nuevo, a bridge that spans the El Tajo Gorge and connects the old and new parts of the city. The bridge was completed in 1793 and offers stunning views of the surrounding countryside. Other notable landmarks in Ronda include the Plaza de Toros, one of the oldest and most historic bullfighting rings in Spain, and the Alameda del Tajo, a beautiful park with stunning views over the gorge.

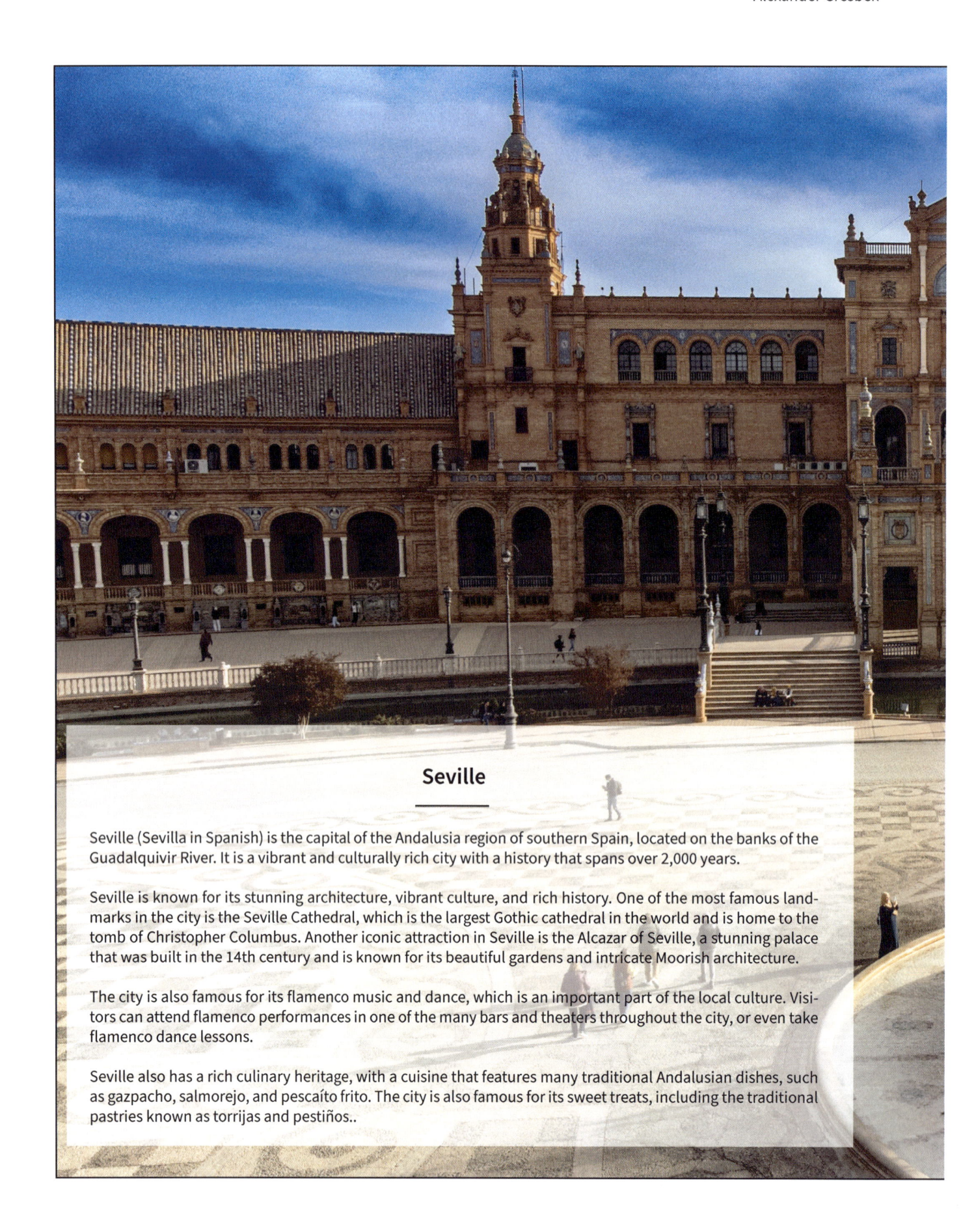

Alexander Gresbek

Seville

Seville (Sevilla in Spanish) is the capital of the Andalusia region of southern Spain, located on the banks of the Guadalquivir River. It is a vibrant and culturally rich city with a history that spans over 2,000 years.

Seville is known for its stunning architecture, vibrant culture, and rich history. One of the most famous landmarks in the city is the Seville Cathedral, which is the largest Gothic cathedral in the world and is home to the tomb of Christopher Columbus. Another iconic attraction in Seville is the Alcazar of Seville, a stunning palace that was built in the 14th century and is known for its beautiful gardens and intricate Moorish architecture.

The city is also famous for its flamenco music and dance, which is an important part of the local culture. Visitors can attend flamenco performances in one of the many bars and theaters throughout the city, or even take flamenco dance lessons.

Seville also has a rich culinary heritage, with a cuisine that features many traditional Andalusian dishes, such as gazpacho, salmorejo, and pescaíto frito. The city is also famous for its sweet treats, including the traditional pastries known as torrijas and pestiños..

Alexander Gresbek

The Plaza de España, Torre del Oro and Metropol Parasol

The Plaza de España is a famous landmark in Seville, Spain. It is located in the Parque de María Luisa, a large park that was originally created as the private garden of the Palace of San Telmo. The plaza was built in 1928 for the Ibero-American Exposition, a world's fair that was held in Seville that year.

The Plaza de España is a stunning example of Renaissance Revival architecture and is considered one of the most beautiful public spaces in Spain.

Torre del Oro: This tower was built in the 13th century and served as a watchtower and defensive structure. It now houses a naval museum.

Metropol Parasol: This modern wooden structure is located in the Plaza de la Encarnación and is the largest wooden structure in the world. Visitors can take an elevator to the top for beautiful views of the city.

Alexander Gresbek

Discovering Spain and the Costa Blanca | 93

Alexander Gresbek

Alexander Gresbek

Torrevieja

Torrevieja is a coastal city located in the province of Alicante, in the Valencian Community of Spain. It is situated on the Mediterranean Sea, approximately 50 kilometers south of the city of Alicante.

The city is known for its beautiful beaches, salt lakes, and mild climate, which makes it a popular destination for tourists and expatriates. Torrevieja has a population of around 80,000 inhabitants.

The salt sea or Las Salinas de Torrevieja, is an important natural attraction in the city of Torrevieja. It is a saltwater lagoon, which covers an area of approximately 1,400 hectares and is located to the south of the city.

Alexander Gresbek

Alexander Gresbek

Valencia

Valencia is located on the eastern coast of Spain, on the banks of the Turia River. It is the third-largest city in Spain, after Madrid and Barcelona, and the capital of the Valencian Community. Valencia has a rich history, with influences from the Romans, Moors, and Christians, and it is known for its stunning architecture, lively culture, and delicious cuisine.

Discovering Spain and the Costa Blanca | 97

City of Arts and Sciences

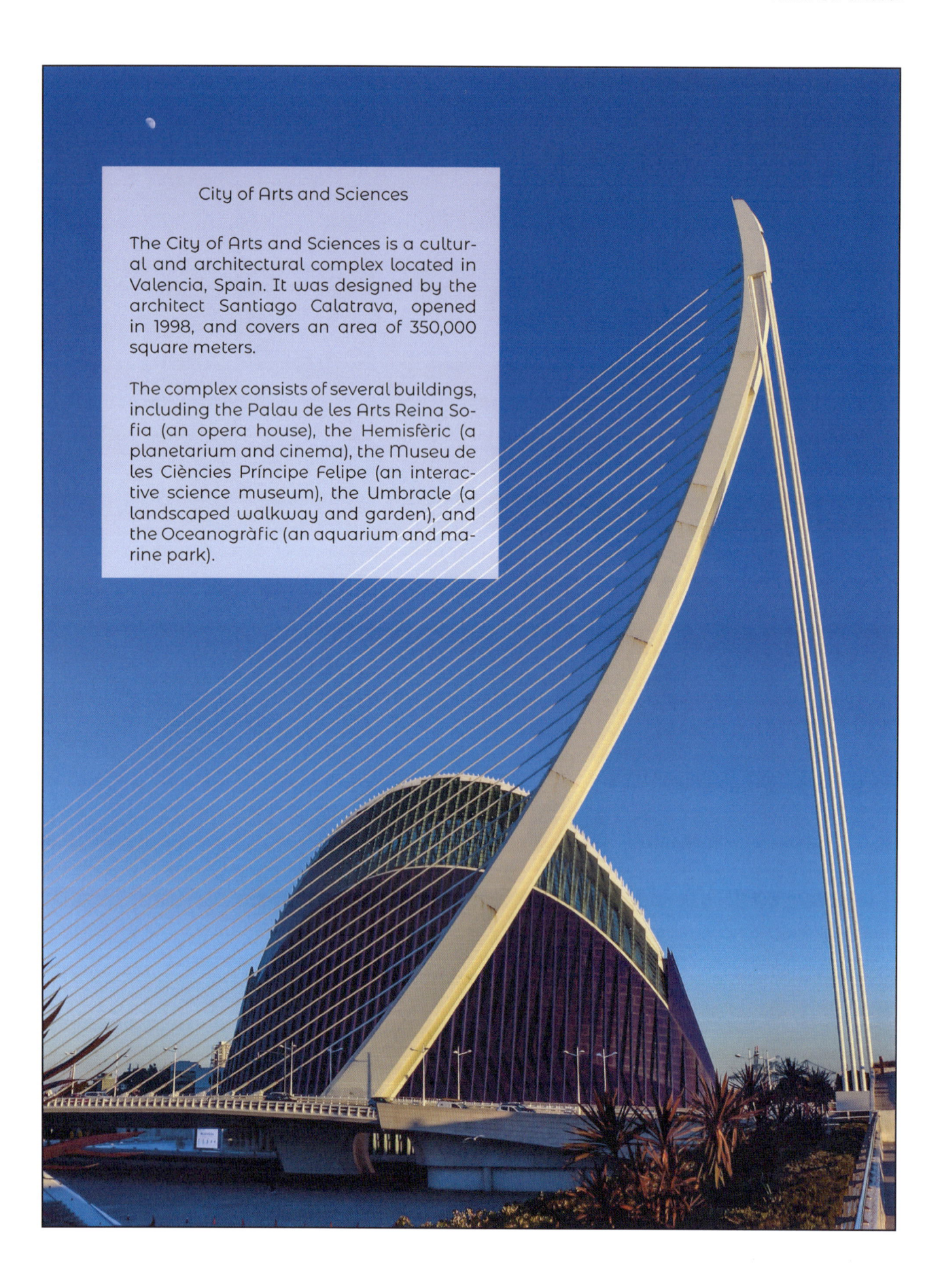

The City of Arts and Sciences is a cultural and architectural complex located in Valencia, Spain. It was designed by the architect Santiago Calatrava, opened in 1998, and covers an area of 350,000 square meters.

The complex consists of several buildings, including the Palau de les Arts Reina Sofia (an opera house), the Hemisfèric (a planetarium and cinema), the Museu de les Ciències Príncipe Felipe (an interactive science museum), the Umbracle (a landscaped walkway and garden), and the Oceanogràfic (an aquarium and marine park).

Alexander Gresbek

Discovering Spain and the Costa Blanca | 99

Alexander Gresbek

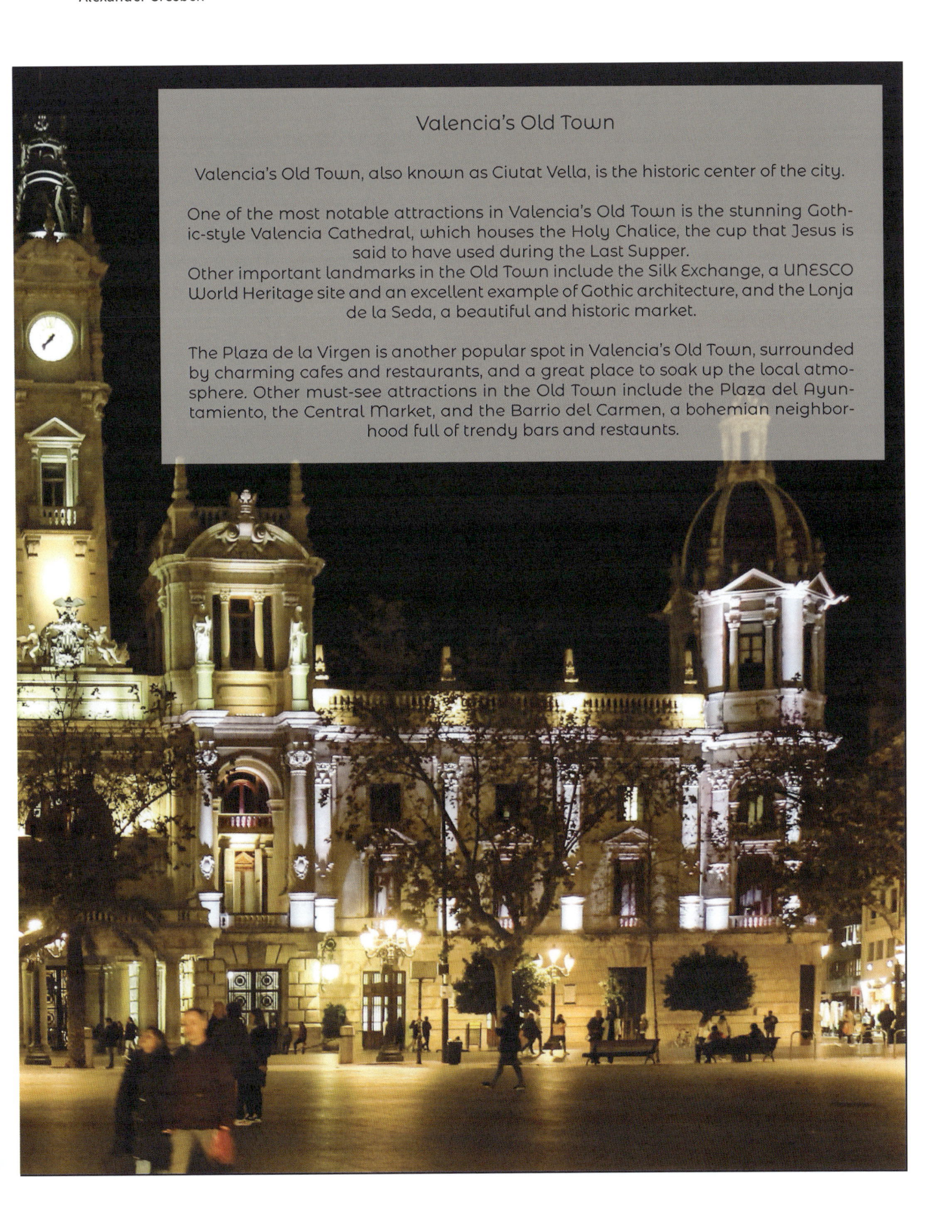

Alexander Gresbek

Valencia's Old Town

Valencia's Old Town, also known as Ciutat Vella, is the historic center of the city.

One of the most notable attractions in Valencia's Old Town is the stunning Gothic-style Valencia Cathedral, which houses the Holy Chalice, the cup that Jesus is said to have used during the Last Supper.
Other important landmarks in the Old Town include the Silk Exchange, a UNESCO World Heritage site and an excellent example of Gothic architecture, and the Lonja de la Seda, a beautiful and historic market.

The Plaza de la Virgen is another popular spot in Valencia's Old Town, surrounded by charming cafes and restaurants, and a great place to soak up the local atmosphere. Other must-see attractions in the Old Town include the Plaza del Ayuntamiento, the Central Market, and the Barrio del Carmen, a bohemian neighborhood full of trendy bars and restaunts.

Alexander Gresbek

Alexander Gresbek

Zaragoza

Zaragoza, also known as Saragossa, is a beautiful and historic city in northeastern Spain. One of the main highlights of the city is the Basilica del Pilar, which is a magnificent baroque church that is considered to be one of the most important religious landmarks in Spain. Located on the banks of the Ebro River, it houses a statue of the Virgin Mary and is a popular destination for visitors.

Alexander Gresbek

———

Alexander Gresbek was born in 1965 in London. After completing his degree in business administration with a focus on marketing and foreign trade, he worked as a manager in the logistics industry in Nuremberg, Düsseldorf and Bonn.

In 2018, he moved with his wife Anuschka to the Costa Blanca, where he works as an author and photographer.

To quote the auther: "I highly recommend that you visit Spain and discover all that it has to offer. From the lively cities like Madrid and Barcelona to the serene beaches of the Costa Blanca, Spain has something for everyone to fall in love with".

Printed in Great Britain
by Amazon